MW01100664

# A Woman's Mind Half Naked

by Jennifer Ann Gordon

Publishing Syndicate
Orangevale, California

# A Woman's Mind Half Naked

First Edition 2011

Copyright 2011 by Jennifer Ann Gordon

Cover and Book Design: Publishing Syndicate
Back Cover Photo: Jennifer Ann Gordon, self-portrait
Photo page 123: Steven Hellon
Book Editor: Terri Elders

ISBN 978-0-9824654-7-9

Library of Congress Control Number 2011908419

Printed in Canada

Published by:     **Publishing Syndicate**
                  **PO Box 607**
                  **Orangevale, CA 95662**
                  **Fax 916-987-6501**
                  **Ken@PublishingSyndicate.com**
                  **www.PublishingSyndicate.com**

*I joyfully dedicate this book to Beautiful Betty. Our last few days together were pure bliss. I love you, BB! Live on.*

# A Woman's Mind Half Naked

**I Love You** **Welcome to my heart's village!**
I want to hear your story, to hold you in my
arms, to listen to you without judgment. I want
us to laugh and cry together. I want to feel
hope with you. It doesn't matter who you are
or where you live, what your job title is or what
lies in your past. We are connected. I care that
you are well and have what you need. I care
that you feel your value and importance in this
family we call humanity.

Writing to you is a fun camping trip. A
solitary trek inward. A chuckle. A hard cry.
An opera. A fabulous meal in a French café.
Lavender honey right from the comb. Standing
barefoot on a packed dirt floor. Dancing with
abandon. More than anything else, writing to
you is my hug filled with hope for our journey
together.

Affectionately,

**Universe Traveler** I am a universe traveler. Yes! I've circled around the sun at the breakneck speed of 67,000 miles per hour quite a few times now. And I've never felt newer or more like a blushing bride of life than I feel right now. After three children, two marriages and a million invaluable lessons and experiences in love, business and staying authentic, I am a self-proclaimed *virgin*.

**A Virgin Again** "Virgin" has a lot of definitions. My favorite is "an uncaptured or unconquered place or thing." I love the idea of being both an *uncaptured* and *unconquered* place. I feel new and strong. I don't care what others think of me . . . mostly. I have learned how not to take things personally. I love open-ended questions. Finally, I understand that life doesn't need to be tied up with a neat little bow or explained. I rejoice in recognizing and challenging my own assumptions.

## Fifty Percent Ain't Bad I'm pretty

secure at least fifty percent of the time. The other fifty is buoyed by precious friends and the fact that I know how to observe my thoughts without fear. I am curious. Joyfully, I share with you that I've had the proverbial shit kicked out of me over the years. Thank goodness. Having traveled from "Good Christian" to "Fallen Angel," from "Great Student" to "College Drop-Out"—you get the gist—I don't regret a thing. I have been freed from the idea that God is keeping score, tallying up points and hovering over my shoulder all the time just waiting to condemn me or pat me on the back. And I am seriously uninterested in going to a club where only a few are welcomed while the bouncers keep everyone else back.

**Freedom Begins** The biggest burden I had to bear over the years during this liberating process was that of my own arrogance. I began my twenties knowing everything about God. Because I knew everything about God, I also knew everything about people, what they should or should not do or what they really needed to be thinking to be more like, ahem, *me*.

I had never questioned anything I was taught about God until age 29 when my dad died. Two days after I found out he was so ill, he was gone. His last words to me? "I am so frightened." My heart broke, and out poured all the questions that had been waiting in the wings. My honest inquiry began.

**Macaroni and Cheese** The macaroni and cheese did it. I opened the refrigerator. It was filled with little dishes of food that my mom had prepared for my dad, trying to get him to eat something . . . *anything*. The macaroni and cheese was crusted over and dried out. I just stared at it. It became my icon for what my marriage felt like. My exact thought was probably a lot like many people's thoughts when they are facing the death of a loved one: *Life is too short to spend being miserable.* I was done. Two months later I separated from my husband.

**Letting Go of the Oars** I stuffed my intuition in a metal box, locked it, and then hid it in the garage behind the recycling. Although I tripped over it on occasion, I never unpacked it fully to polish and place on my heart's mantel. Had a beautiful baby girl. Got married again. Had two glorious baby boys. Almost died of a broken heart. More stuff happened. I became a single full-time mom and breadwinner with no college degree, no job, no place to live, no money, no car and no confidence. My life was a canvas. I moved forward brushstroke by brushstroke. I began to spread my sail to let the wind power me, rather than frantically rowing my boat in circles.

**Angels with Arms** **My favorite fortune** cookie message is this: *It is better to be angel with arms than angel with wings.* I call kind people *Angels-with-Arms*. The angel-director of the preschool who pulled me aside to tell me my one- and four-year-old sons could attend gratis. The angel-gentleman at church who had an extra car I could "test drive" for six months. Then there was the angel-director of the YMCA who gave me a big hug, refused my offer to work in exchange for a membership and then gave me a full year's membership free and clear. My angel-brother and angel-friends. Angel-artists and angel-authors, too. Angel-grandma. Angel-landlords and angel-clients.

A special mention must be given to *Angels-by-Inverse*, those dear folks who made my life so difficult that I had to dig deep within for strength, to seek help rather than be my normally reclusive self.

My life is truly a testament to the compassion, kindness and generosity of most people. Each day overflows with love and brilliance. It really does take an entire village of angels to raise a child.

## Gratitude Saves My Neck I roll out

my red carpet every day for interesting people, thoughts, ideas, inspiration, music, art, books and other sumptuous gifts to walk into my life. During both great and seriously difficult times, gratitude is my lifeline to sanity and balance. Yep, my red carpet is gratitude. I run, skip, hop on one foot or sashay down this carpet joyfully to greet the moment. Sometimes I cry en route to gratitude.

This is how it works. (Note: most of this I learned by inverse.) Rather than make reactionary decisions based on what I don't have, gratitude grounds me and lets me begin with a positive . . . what I have on hand.

The *bigmoment*, my epiphany—to always begin with gratitude—splashed me when I was at my lowest point. Life seemed too hard. I was depressed. I was so sad. Just as I fantasized driving into a big oak tree at a hundred miles per hour, my plan of action unfurled before my very eyes: *Look for every little good thing around you. Make your days an endless treasure hunt for the beautiful, the delightful, the loving.* It felt good to have a plan of action.

I began immediately. When I started to get depressed again, I'd look for even more good, even if I started with something really small like, "I am glad I put the toilet paper on the holder, rather than let it sit on the floor by the toilet." Or, "I am *thankyoufull* there is air." Just about anything to break the fear inertia and get my gratitude momentum rolling.

Gratitude leads to creative solutions. Gratitude is the precursor to abundance and harmony. Borrowing from American Express, "I never leave home without it."

# Beautiful Husbands Everywhere

Jerry and his wife, Moni, are among my favorite neighbors. We have a *happywavinghello* relationship sprinkled with the occasional chat on the road. I treasure my moments with them.

One morning, and for the first time ever, Jerry knocked on my door. He was on a mission. Through our high-speed country neighborhood grapevine (which puts the fastest Internet connectivity to shame) Jerry had heard that one of our other neighbors was less than polite to me. This Angel-by-Inverse is notorious in our small neighborhood community for his violent outbursts and irrational behavior. My son's trumpet playing had annoyed this man and he tromped to my front door to launch a full verbal assault on my character and parenting skills, especially me being a single mother.

Angel-Jerry's mission: "Jennifer, I came over to tell you that you are a wonderful mom! Your children have restored my faith in children. What he did was illegal. If anyone approached and talked to my wife the way he talked to you, I would have shot him. If he ever sets one foot on your property again, call the sheriff."

At this precise moment, it hit me. My husband is . . . many men. I have beautiful husbands everywhere. For far too long, I entertained the sorrowful misconceptions that I needed a husband, and also that I had no husband. Not true on either account.

Every day holds many gallant, thoughtful, protective and tender expressions by many men in my professional life and personal circles, and even complete strangers. Someday I'll have to write a book entitled *My Husbands*.

# My Grocery-Store Husband

Several years ago, I'd reached a very difficult time in my life. My children and I had just been evicted in retaliation for my insistence that our landlord keep his promises of repair. To top this off, we had a dog that went berserk whenever she was away from me. I had no choice but to turn the dog in to the animal shelter. She had been my hiking buddy and my constant companion. My heart turned to dust. I watched her watch me leave her. I cried uncontrollably.

I needed to go to the grocery store, but dreaded what I call the "gauntlet of kindness." I prayed that no one ask me if I needed help finding something, or how I was, as I was in danger of losing my tenuous composure and crying again. Much to my dismay, the manager approached and asked, "How are you today?" With my lips pursed, I replied, "Can't talk, will cry." The manager responded, "Oh, what's wrong?" At that point I lost it completely. Tears streamed down my face. My nose ran. I had the dry heaves. I told him my story.

Then he did something extraordinary. He held open his arms. I went to him. He wrapped his arms around me tightly and didn't let go for what seemed to be a very long time. I held on for dear life. I got snot and tears and drool all over his shoulder.

When I calmed down, he said, "Look at me. You did the right thing. Everything is going to be all right. You are a remarkable woman. You did the right thing." This man's compassion greatly comforted me. My *grocery-store husband* gave me hope.

As I continued with my shopping, he chased me with handfuls of soft pink tissue. "I thought you might need these," he said. Although I never saw him again, his act of kindness stayed with me and helped long after that day.

**Sunglasses** I was disgruntled. I paid a lot of money for my family to watch the movie and the screen was so dark. The projectionist should have checked the bulbs *before* the movie! I sat through it agitated. The movie ended. I fully intended to talk to the manager to get a refund. Then I realized that I had, ahem, forgotten to remove my sunglasses.

The dark picture had nothing to do with the theater, the actors, the producer, the projector or the projectionist. In fact, the dim lighting had nothing to do with anybody else but me. I could have easily fixed the problem by taking off my sunglasses.

This leads me to an obvious metaphor: what filter are we gazing through? When one of our life-movies is lackluster, dark or dim, the first thing we should check is to see whether we have removed our own preconceptions, opinions and assumptions in order to see the colorful rendering called *Life.*

**Easier Said Than Done** Right. Take
the sunglasses off. Remove preconceptions,
assumptions and opinions from our view.
How? Curiosity. Curiosity never killed
*this* cat! Curiosity puts us in a state of
receptiveness to a new viewpoint, a deeper
understanding and fuller compassion.

Curiosity is listening without judgment.
Curiosity is giving others the encourage-
ment and room they need to tell their stories. Curiosity asks questions rather than
categorizes and labels. Curiosity replaces
fear. Curiosity makes life fun!

I've always loved Rudyard Kipling's *The
Elephant's Child* with his " 'satiable curtios-
ity." No matter how many times his elders
spanked him for asking too many questions,
he remained curious. Finally, his curiosity,
which almost got him eaten by a crocodile,
ended up stretching his "blackish, bulgy
nose as big as a boot" into a long and very
useful trunk with which he spanked all
those who had spanked him so unmercifully
for being insatiably curious.

**Time Bender** **I am a time bender. As**
the sole parent of three children, I haven't
taken many vacations. But I am an expert at
gleaning two weeks worth of rejuvenation
in a few hours, or a two-day respite in one
hour. I can deeply imbibe inspiration in one
minute or less. I have a system.

I used to think that if I wanted to paint
or read a book or do anything else that
stimulates and rejuvenates me, I needed
fat chunks of time. The problem was that
I never had fat chunks of time. I only had
moments. So I didn't feed myself spiritu-
ally, artistically, intellectually or physically
because, well, I didn't have time. I plumped
up. I was dissatisfied. Hooked up with the
wrong guys. Then I subjected my approach
to intense scrutiny.

Aha! That I needed large swaths of time
was the leading misconception. I decided to
conduct an ongoing experiment to use my
unproductive minutes creatively. I began to

carry a book with me at all times. In line at the grocery store? I read. Waiting for kids at the dentist? Out came my book. I left my art and photography books open all over the house. I changed the page a couple of times each day. Ten seconds with Van Gogh's *Starry Night* put a tiger in my tank. Soon I was infusing my life and my days with inspiration, knowledge and joy. And I'm still going strong.

## Tahoe Two Hours = Vacation²

One of my most restful vacations was a mere two hours in South Lake Tahoe, only an hour's drive from my home. A friend and I rented banana-shaped kayaks and floated naked on the lake. We were both exhausted from long days with very little rest. We took naked naps to the water lapping its lullaby.

When I awoke, I felt completely rested and ready to roll. Two weeks at a resort could not have been more rejuvenating. You get the idea. I'm still learning, refining and designing. I don't plan on halting my time-bending experiment ever!

**The Magic Car** There I was, minding
my own business, driving along and thinking
about all sorts of things. What a great time
I had with my mom that morning, how
excited I was about my new job, how glad I
was to be heading out to have dinner with a
friend. Sex was not on my mind. Both of my
hands were firmly planted on the steering
wheel at ten and two o'clock. The road was
not extra-bumpy.

All of a sudden, I felt funny. Funny as in
. . . close to orgasm. I looked at the cars and
trucks all around me, worried that somehow their drivers could tell what was going
on in my southern parts. No one seemed to
notice anything unusual.

Then fireworks exploded, music cre-
scendoed, flower petals floated dreamily
down . . . for the next half hour! With no
premeditation or conscious personal over-
lay (pun intended), I began to scream. I kept
checking traffic to make sure everything was

groovy and my *weirdbutglorious* adventure remained undetected.

An O to top all O's, and no one else was with me. Furthermore, the only reason the Big O subsided when I arrived at the restaurant was that I had to get out of the car and walk into the restaurant to meet my friend. I used all the control I could muster to calm down.

Dinner was pleasant. Afterward, I got back into my car and then it started again. Three days later, it subsided somewhat, even though it still lurked in the shadows just waiting to spring into action. Business as usual was quite challenging, like going through the day's duties on a pogo stick.

So I conducted an informal survey with my closest girlfriends. Has this ever happened to you? One answered, "No, but I'm jealous. If you figure it out, let me know how I can get some, OK?"

**Ode to LA** **I really like LA. For me,**
Hollywood, Venice, Santa Monica are all
Los Angeles. My apologies. After all, I am
a Northern Californian. We don't even
acknowledge SoCal's right to be part of our
state.

The combined fragrances of smog and
salty ocean air delight me. The big swing
sets on the beach . . . well, there is nothing
better than to swing way up high to kiss the
sky and the sea's horizon.

What really thrills me about LA is the
creative energy there, the derring-do, the
people who are risking all to live their pas-
sions. In LA, the artist in me blooms. The
rebel in me surges. And the lover of humanity smiles at the diversity and blows kisses
to everyone I meet. The playfulness of LA,
the music, the craziness . . . things are hop-
pin' there.

**Ass on a Hot Grill** "What burns my ass on a hot grill is that we think all this is tied to our worth," said AuntJo.

My friend AuntJo lives in Texas. I was stressed, so I called her to spill my angst and get a bit of perspective. I talked. I cried. AuntJo listened. Most of my anxiety was about money, or so I thought.

"AuntJnfr [Jennifer]," AuntJo said, "This isn't about money. This is about worth."

I knew she was right the minute she said it. So often we think our job, money in the bank and others' opinion—all external labels and facts—give us our identity.

I had been anxious about proving my worth to a colleague. AuntJo's words of wisdom struck a home run and I felt calm once again.

# Aftermath of a Bath for a Laugh

Last night, I decided to take a long, hot bath. I put lavender oil and a luxurious ball of *somethingelse* guaranteed to give a glow to my skin into the inviting, steamy water. Lovely.

Then I decided I would give my digits a French manicure while I soaked. Painting my fingernails even under ideal conditions is probably my worst subject beauty-wise, worse than putting on red lipstick. It's difficult enough all dry and wearing my glasses. Trying to give myself a manicure in the tub *sans* my glasses was just asking for trouble. But I forgot about that. "The trouble with you, Jennifer," Grandma used to say, "is that you are an idealist. You usually think in best-case scenarios."

With four fingernails done sloppily, I reached to dip my teeny fingernail polish paintbrush into the jar of polish. The open jar fell into the bath water. I retrieved it.

There wasn't too much water in the jar, so I continued. Soon I noticed that there was a weird fingernail polish slick in my bathtub. When I emerged from my soak, I was marbled! Faux painted! *Trompe l'oeil.* Michelangelo's *Jennifer*.

Then I looked at my fingernails and they were all gooey and marbled, too. So I cleaned up, slopped some clear polish on the once gooey windshields of my *doigts* (*fingers*, in French) and called it a manicure.

**Baking Bread** Life is a lot like baking bread. This hit me recently when I was feeling restless and unprofitably wedged. My business. My own lust for life and love. It seemed that I was at a crossroads . . . again. Possibly on the verge of failure or great success depending. The one thing I knew is that I was a very discouraged entrepreneur.

I sat at my favorite café. Stuck, I pulled out my notebook and began to write questions to which there were no answers. Blah, blah, blah. I quit writing.

Suddenly my pen went crazy. "Let it rise" emblazoned itself across my legal pad. Then my pen sketched a delicious, crusty loaf of French bread. Okay, sister. I get it. Life is a lot like making bread.

I've really put the highest quality ingredients into my business and my life, except for the teaspoon of self-doubt now and then: my pure and vibrant desires to contribute to the world, my passion, talents, hard work, compassion, humanity and affection. I've kneaded the dough until its consistency is smooth and elastic.

Here is what I learned: when I don't know what to do, just LET it all rise. TRUST alchemy. *Then* BAKE, turn up the heat. EAT. SHARE. SMILE. Make more bread.

**RSVP** **Recently, a friend asked me what** the acronym RSVP stood for. *Respondez-Vous, S'il Vous Plait.* Or, simply, "Please respond." This lit a flame in me. RSVP. Let's respond to one another and see our bounty grow! People forget their connections to all others and fail to respond, but what else is there really?

For example, I was waiting for an outside table at a local restaurant. A woman with a strikingly graphic black-and-white print sarong swooshed around her shoulders made her way painfully down the steps. Her frustration with her physical challenges and embarrassment were evident in her expression as she reached the last step. RSVP. I smiled and sincerely told her how beautiful and dramatic she looked in her sarong . . . that she had fabulous style. She forgot to be embarrassed or frustrated. Her spirit lifted. RSVP.

Another time, I was struggling with feeling overwhelmed by parenting responsibilities. I pushed my shopping cart laden with groceries to the car. A gentleman watched me approach the car and then asked me if I would let him load everything into my car for me. He took the greatest of care. He asked me to sit inside and do nothing! By the time he had finished, I felt refreshed. He waved and left. RSVP.

**Traveling Inside Out** **I have always**
refused to adopt the mindset of a tourist.
When I first visited France, I decided that
I was not going to go as if I were visiting
an aquarium to gaze at little French fish. I
wanted to feel my connection with those
around me. I wanted to experience France
from the inside out, to make new friends.

Through no effort of my own, I ended
up staying with French friends of friends
who spoke little or no English. I spent a lot
of time with children, bought baguettes,
picked mushrooms in the forest with
Père Robert, listened to Ton-ton Léon and
his wife Mireille sing old French vaude-
ville songs, rode on the back of a scooter
through Paris and so much more. Everyone
rolled out their red carpets. I ate the best
food, prepared fresh from the garden. The
little pastry truck made its rounds and I was
sent out to choose the day's bread and the
morning's pastries. *Heavenonearth*. Bowls

of steaming *café au lait* with sugar cubes. Flaky croissants. Strawberry jam.

Every moment in France was precious and generous. Warm and sweet. Colorful and curious.

**Packed Dirt Floor When I first entered**
the Pueblo Reservation in Taos, New Mexico,
I felt extremely uncomfortable. Standing
there, I quickly identified my discomfort as
coming from a sense of separateness and
observation rather than feeling one beating
heart. There I was . . . uninspired. It felt
unholy, almost to the point of unbearable,
to look upon the Pueblo people and culture
as curiosities or as separate from myself. I
couldn't make myself enter the shops.

I stood by the brook listening. All of a
sudden I had to be barefoot. I had to stand
barefoot on that dirt where the Pueblo Indi-
ans had walked for thousands of years!

I found a quiet, shady spot between
homes and kicked off my shoes and socks,
unaware that I was being observed. The
dirt felt cool and comfortable. "Feel better now?" asked an artist from his shop.
"Much," I replied.

I spent the entire afternoon in joy, wan-
dering barefoot in the pueblo.

**Live Sexy** I have friends who own an
organic lavender farm. They distill their own
essential oils and create natural beauty and
aromatherapy products from their harvests.
Yiannis and Karen are bounty, boldness,
harvest and celebration . . . and fragrant,
gorgeous living. Some of my sexiest life
experiences to date have been with these
two on their estate.

Yiannis chose the property because it
was so much like his homeland in Sparta,
Greece. He and Karen created their dream.
Old olive trees line the winding way up to
their house. An organic heirloom tomato
garden. An organic vineyard with antique
roses growing at the end of each row. A
huge vegetable garden. Greek wine. Lavender *crème brulée*. Lavender barbecued
salmon. Laughter. Fountains. Over nine
thousand lavender plants. Grapes plucked
from the vine, juice running down chins and
arms. Tomatoes warmed by the sun, eaten

right there in the garden. Sigh.

One summer afternoon, Yiannis and I walked along the rows of lavender. I was wearing minimal summer clothing and could feel the sun bathing my shoulders, and caressing the back of my neck and legs. I told Yiannis that I would like to lie down in between the rows of lavender and be still, to just listen. He understood completely and left.

There were thousands, no, millions of bees of all shapes, sizes and frequencies buzzing around the lavender blossoms. I lay down. Looking up through the lavender plants, I listened to this *Symphony of Bees.* I didn't think at all. The fragrance, music, sunshine, bees and me! Something clicked. Live life sexy! Enjoy! Pay attention!

**Honey** **I sat in Karen and Yiannis' kitchen** talking with Karen while she prepared her amazing gourmet fare. Karen is an artist. She creates fabulous, fresh, beautiful meals. Karen is my *patron saint of artful food*. She inspires me to live beautifully and bountifully.

As Karen and I cavorted and chortled, Yiannis walked in. He held a tray with honeycomb dripping with lavender honey. Pulling his ever-present broad-bladed knife from its sheath on his belt, he cut a chunk of honeycomb and gestured for me to take it. "Eat. Take it in your fingers. Eat the comb, too."

I received this sweet, drippy gift and ate it. Then I licked my fingers. That honey tasted like life. Another sexy life moment with these two dear friends. Life really is feeding others honey straight from our heart-hives. And receiving comb from the broad-bladed knife of a friend. Licking our fingers. Laughing.

**Sex & Sausages** Ever see women mobilize? Women seem to know intuitively how to work together to create an environment of warmth for maximum cavorting and chortling.

Sex & Sausages, an all-girl version of Oktoberfest. Fire in the fireplace. Four women in the kitchen cooking bratwurst and drinking Cosmos and stout ale, and juice for those who were abstaining for whatever reason.

Where does the "sex" come in? We all watched the movie Sex and the City. Leslie kept us grounded. "Those women are so spoiled," she said. "Yes," we all agreed. I defended the movie for the fun fashion and because the character Carrie was a writer. We all pontificated about the traditional male stereotypes transposed to their female equivalents in the movie. We got smarter and smarter as our glasses emptied and our bellies filled.

I cherish these women. Somehow, we have created a deeply safe environment where we can be ourselves, listen to one another without judgment, pull together when someone is suffering and laugh a lot.

Our next all-femme bash will have a pirate theme, replete with eye-patches, telescopes, compasses, parrots and skull-and-crossbones flags. But what food should I serve?

**Women Pirates** I could really be a pirate if I just weren't so sweet. Yep, my sweetness is a big problem to my piratey badself. Aargh! Admittedly, I do have pirate thoughts sometimes. These times are usually in business when I witness the good ol' boy network, when I see women being cruel to women or when children are treated unkindly. But I digress. Back to women pirates.

Women pirates. Fascinating. Leaders. Lovers. Derring-do. Undaunted in the face of danger. Women of action. They were fierce and fabulous in their own right. Historically, they plundered/defended what society didn't allow women to possess. My take is that they were fed up being put in their places and decided to take action.

Some of these femme pirates are fairly contemporary. Huang P'ei-mei led fifty thousand pirates in China from 1937 to the mid-50s. Pirate Linda operated in the Philippines as late as the 1980s.

There needs to be an epic movie about women pirates. Perhaps I'll write one.

**Aha  Every day holds so much** *aha* potential. The last ten minutes of most meaningful conversations usually contain the *aha*. So stay with it.

If I were to write *aha* instructions, they'd read: don't be afraid to amble or to be tangential. *Aha*s rarely, if ever, come in a linear fashion. *Aha*s love to surprise us. *Aha*s are the harmonious, exciting and sudden convergence of seemingly disjointed concepts or information. Spiral inward. Spiral outward. Sashay. Wiggle your hips. Listen intently. Ask "what if?" Enjoy the journey.

In business circles, an *aha*-approach is often referred to as "thinking outside the box." However, I like the idea of obliterating the box entirely. There is no box. Box and thinking don't belong in the same sentence.

**Ferch Arbennig** I collect words like some people collect stamps or teacups or coins. My dear friend James is from Wales. One day his e-salutation to me was "Ferch Arbennig," the approximate pronunciation of which is "Vechhhh Ar-BAY-neg." It sounds so much better when James says it.

*Ferch Arbennig* means "special girl" in Welsh. I liked this phrase so much that I graffitied it on my jeans in fat letters down the front of the right leg. I want to create a worldwide *Ferch Arbennig* club! Truly yours, F.A.

**Ligamota** When AuntJo lived in Norway, she learned the language by total immersion. Many of the word and phrases she learned she never saw in writing so she had no idea how to spell them.

As we were ending a phone conversation, I told AuntJo that I loved her. She replied, "Ligamota." (Or, at least, that's how it sounded to me.) Then she explained that *ligamota* meant *rightbackatyou* in Norwegian.

*Ligamota* became our special word. Frankly, it sounded like Japanese rather than Norwegian to me, which demonstrates my unfathomable void of understanding of both Norwegian and Japanese.

Then I almost dated a Norwegian. He said that he was looking forward to having lunch with me. I replied, "Ligamota." He was thrilled. He knew exactly what it meant.

I seized the opportunity to ask him how to spell this special phrase. L-e-i-g-h m-o-d-e. That's what I said, "*Ligamota*."

## **Comforting Java Joy** Times were

rough. I felt pretty much like roadkill, a flattened carcass with my tail blowing in the breeze.

Hope shows up, though, when we're ready to receive it. This time hope arrived in a cup of coffee. I was barely awake when I heard a light knock on my bedroom door. My precious friend Molly entered with a steaming cup of French roast with cream.

Someone was serving *me* coffee in bed? Wow! Her gentle gesture made me feel like royalty, a cherished guest bathed in honor and care. Even now, whenever I need to feel more confident and expectant of good, the moment of being served that beautiful cup of coffee in bed returns and comforts me.

Over the years, I've learned that this is Molly's way of being. She is full of grace and the very best kind of surprises.

**Kristiana** I met Kristiana while we were both in line at the food court waiting to place our orders. The cashier asked the woman at the front of the line, "What's on your mind?" I mumbled under my breath, "That's a loaded question."

Kristiana, who was in front of me, turned around and asked me, "What is on your mind?" I replied, "Men." She responded, "Me, too!" And that's all it took. Fast friends for life. Even better, I found out she lived just a few miles from me.

Several years later, I sent Kristiana a copy of this manuscript to be a test-reader. She had just read the chapter "Comforting Java Joy" and e-mailed to tell me that her husband "G" brings her coffee in bed every morning. I'm still smiling.

**Giotto and Mom** **My mom and I, along** with a 13th century Italian artist and architect by the name of Giotto di Bondone, had a fabulous time together a few years ago. In fact, it was from this tea party with Mom and Giotto that I learned the potential my mom and I had to enjoy one another.

Both Mom and I are artists. Ever since I can remember, art has been our one safe meeting place or common ground.

Mom had injured her foot and was relegated to the couch. We sat snuggled up for hours with her enormous book of Giotto's work in our laps, talking about each dramatic drawing. We were asking questions. Equality, curiosity and listening with love were rare in our relationship. I soaked it in.

Giotto became my friend that day. Not only do I love his bold style and his ability for details and vibrant pictorial storytelling, he's now a happy connection to my mom. I still turn to him for insight and inspiration, too. His style grounds and emboldens me. But mostly, Giotto reminds me how harmony with Mom feels.

What a dreamy afternoon!

## **Captain Krang** The problem was that

Captain Krang loved only Claire. When Claire first introduced us, the good captain was subdued and, while not accepting, tolerant.

The first nervous night we spent together, we sat at opposite ends of the couch. I held my dinner plate in my lap. Every few minutes, I threw a piece of chicken over to the good Captain. We bonded.

The next day, he actually let me pet him and soon we were cronies. I always made sure that I was very communicative, quiet and gentle with the dear Captain.

Two months later, Claire and her family returned home. She asked me *whatonearth* I had done to Captain Krang! "I've never seen him so calm and content," she said.

Also *after* she returned home, she shared that before me she hadn't been able to find a dog-sitter who was willing to stay with the Captain because he was so *unpredictable.* Frankly, I'm glad she hadn't shared this with me beforehand. I smiled.

Sometimes, the best relationships, even with Schnauzers, are the ones that require great care and move like a deep, slow river, rather than a torrent.

**Big Yellow Pyramids** **A new version** of swimming came into my life when I committed to training for a triathlon with an all-women team.

Before training for this triathlon at age forty-nine, I had never swum in a straight line. I played in the water. Pulled a chain of children all holding hands and feet around in circles. Stood on my hands. Practiced holding my breath. Took turns singing songs underwater and trying to identify the song, an aqua version of *Name That Tune*. I still play, but I've fallen in lust with *swimming in a straight line* . . . mostly.

By the time the event arrived, I was mentally prepared, thanks to my coaches and fellow teammates. My mantra was, "*Complete, don't compete*," which was de-signed to calm me down and help me keep my eye on the goal.

While I doubted my readiness—I need-ed ten more weeks of training, at least—I knew I had to buck up, take the plunge and finish.

My station was set up. Bike facing outward in the bicycle rack. A pan full of water to step into to rinse the sand off my feet, with a little towel to dry them before putting on my socks and cycling shoes. Bicycle helmet. Sunglasses. Cycling gloves. Sports drinks. Socks. Running shoes. Cycling shoes. All my *tri-accoutrements* were laid out for maximum efficiency.

The swim was the first stage. I gazed out at the lake. The course was marked with giant yellow pyramid-shaped buoys. The swimmers entered the water. I lagged a bit to avoid the flailing arms and feet. Then I took the plunge. My inner gyroscope was on alert. Any doubts I had previously about whether or not I'd be able to complete the swim vanished. My North Star was that first big yellow pyramid buoy. I kept it in sight, never deviating from my course. Another swimmer accidentally clunked me on the head with his arm.

"Sorry," he said.

"No worries," I replied.

I regained my composure and my bearings and continued on. Rounding the first yellow pyramid, I focused on the second yellow pyramid in the middle of the lake. This was easier because the sun was out of my eyes. I became more determined as I rounded the second pyramid. Straight as an arrow, I swam for the neon orange markers on the beach. My hands hit the sand. I stood up and ran.

The bicycling and running parts of the triathlon that followed were tough. At times I doubted if I were going to hold up to the end. My coach ran with me part of the way to keep me going. But I persevered. I sprinted across the finish line into my brother's arms.

Those big, yellow pyramids taught me

something that I had read about, but hadn't fully realized until that point: when the goal is measurable and in sight, it's so much easier to reach it and have a great time doing so!

After completing the triathlon, I realized that I had filled my life with endless and invisible goals, that I never knew where I was regarding *anything.* These nebulous goals were a lot like laundry. Just as one load is completed, another load of dirty clothes has been mysteriously generated. With laundry, I never feel as if I really accomplish anything.

Now I try to make sure that I have *Big Yellow Pyramids* for everything I undertake so I stay on course, reach my goals and have something to celebrate.

**Cyclops My son Jacob bought a book on** ventriloquism. This book was filled mostly with suggestions for all the mischievous pranks one can pull once ventriloquism is mastered. And with this book came a prop—a little pair of plastic eyeballs connected with a bent piece of plastic like the nose-bridge on a pair of glasses. Evidently such eyeballs are must-have for any budding ventriloquist who begins by creating a character-puppet with his hand. Of course, this character needs to see!

Before school one morning, I saw Jacob slip the eyeballs into his pocket. I asked, "You're going to get in some trouble today, aren't you?" He calmly replied, "Yes."

He took the eyeballs to school, put them in place on his hand, which served as his puppet, and entertained his classmates while the teacher was trying to instruct. The teacher got angry, broke the eyeball prop in half and threw it away.

When she wasn't looking, he went through her trash, but could find only one of the eyes. He put this eye in his pocket and now his puppet-hand is a Cyclops named Frederic. He thinks the entire episode is hilarious.

The challenging thing is that I think it's funny, too, even though I shouldn't.

**Dymaxion** **Buckminster Fuller used the** word *dymaxion* as a brand name for many of his inventions. "Dynamic" plus "maximum" plus "ion." *Dymaxion* means *maximum advantage with minimum expenditure of energy and material.* Dymaxion. True conservation. The perfect business goal. A way of living. The opposite of stinginess or fear. So exciting!

I wanted to name my company "Dymaxion *something*," but it was already taken. So I asked my Web designer—an amazing inventor, musician and artist in his own right—what he thought about "Dynamic Maximum, Inc."

"Ugh, Jennifer! Buckminster Fuller devoted his life to finding dymaxion solutions to global problems. *Dynamic Maximum* is going in reverse. You've just re-complicated something Bucky devoted his life to . . . eliminating waste."

**Hideout** **For nearly four years I had an** art studio on the second floor of a barn. Hay doors opened out to the countryside with a view of the snow-covered Sierra Nevada. There was a lot of room to paint really big paintings. No heat or cooling system. Sweet little bats decided to hibernate in the sleeves of my paint-splattered green silk jacket I kept hanging on a nail in the studio.

I lose all track of time when I am painting. In the winter, I tended to paint with vibrant tropical colors to keep warm, painting for hours without a break, feeling no cold. But when that painting was complete, when it was time to clean brushes and leave the studio, I'd realize I was frozen.

In the summer, my acrylics would turn to dry rubber on my palette. It was so hot that rivers of sweat would run off the tip of my nose, elbows and from under my breasts. I didn't mind one bit. I wore only a sarong around my waist. Turned on some opera or whatever music I was feeling at the moment. And often I chose to create in sacred silence.

Sometimes I invited friends to have coffee with me in the studio. It was a special kind of secret fort. I brought my percolator out there, along with some cream and cookies, and we'd have a great time.

I really loved that studio! It was separated from the house by fifty yards or so. I liked listening to the children ask each other where I was. They checked all the rooms in the house. Eventually, their voices would get closer to my studio. Finally, one of them would look up through the hay doors and say, "There you are! We've been looking all over for you!"

## **Scrutiny Mutiny** It's easy to get

tangled up inside a painting while creating it. To lose perspective and overdo until the power of the expression is dulled or killed. When I was in my teens, I discovered a way to tell if a painting or drawing worked or not, it if were finished or not.

I hold my drawings and paintings up to the mirror. If the reflection feels complete and balanced, no matter which way I hold the work to the mirror, then I joyfully abandon the painting.

Looking at a reflection in the mirror provides the necessary separation between creator and creation. I'm sure that someone has written a thesis about this, but I don't really care. I know that it works for me.

Yes. When I hold my artwork up to a mirror, the painting is looking back at me! I become the artwork under scrutiny! Is this, ahem, *scrutiny-mutiny*? (Sorry, I couldn't help myself.) I so enjoy my twisty adventure of art and reflection.

**Crunch** **Life needs crunch. Life without** crunch is like crème brulée without the crunchy thin layer of burnt sugar on top. While the crème is good, it needs that delicious crunch of the brulée to be a fabulous dessert.

Crunch is simple. Crunch is definitive. No one can undo a crunch. Crunch is the result of some action. Maximum crunch needs ordinary moments to be fully appreciated.

My life is crunchy. Just the way I like it. I fill my *everyday* with crunches of all sorts.

My favorite crunch is the rhythmic crunch of snowshoes mingled with breathing at high altitude. It's the perfect percussion. *Crunch-inhale-crunch-inhale-crunch.* Warm breath hitting cold air. Little clouds that hang in front of my face for just a moment.

## **Snowshoes** Snowshoes are magical

crunch. Snowshoes are freedom. They keep an explorer from sinking into the stream beneath the snow or falling into the hole around the tree while she unveils her wild heart in wild places.

What are my life's snowshoes? What allows me to engage fully, but not sink into my environment and get stuck?

My life's snowshoes are my good habit of stimulating my creativity every day. I'm an expert at incorporating into my daily routine those things I need to feed my creativity.

For example, I rise really early to partake of the quiet "dark morning," as my daughter used to call it, to center myself, to remember my dreams and to know that I can achieve them. To remember my connection to all else.

I've carved out a reading time, too. Ah, books! I must read everyday. I hang out with people of like hearts and unlike minds. World news and people provide me with diverse perspectives, new insights and lots and lots of ideas.

When I forget to do this, I am quite fortunate to find myself upside down in the snow. Then I right myself, brush the cold from my being and *crunch* on.

**The Starbuckians** My kids and I had just moved from the San Francisco Bay Area to a small town in the Sierra Nevada foothills.

While the kids were in school, I often wrote at Starbucks just to be around other adults. At the time this was *it,* the only Starbucks around, the hot spot for the town's singles and teens and senior citizens and most everybody else.

Jokingly, I called this Starbucks *'Bucks* because, although Starbucks strives for the utmost consistency in its customer experience, this particular store felt quite different. It was filled with the plaid of hunters, the snow boots of skiers en route to the ski resorts up the mountain and with kayakers, local lawyers and a group of men I called the *Starbuckians*.

The *Starbuckians* were the welcoming committee to all new female "regulars." They were men between the ages of 30 and 110 who welcomed any woman willing to put up with their stories about how fabulous and fascinating they were. I liked the *Starbuckians* for their reliability. Generally they were in the same seats at the same times everyday.

## Planet Starbuckia: Ewwwww! One

summer morning I sat outside on the patio at *'Bucks*, sipping my adjective-laden, custom-concocted cup of java. One of the flawlessly regular *Starbuckians* joined me. "I like women with little boobies," he said. He didn't notice my slack jaw. He had no idea the umbrage I, a woman, and a voluptuous one at that, had taken. I asked myself *whatonearth* is it about me that invites men to tell me such bizarre things?

His subsequent narcissistic monologues filled me in on many more details about his life than I had ever wanted to know. After frequenting that Starbucks store for three years, I knew all about his self-perceived accomplishments, about his children, his mother, his dad's little gems of wisdom and his ex-wife.

After three years of lopsided conversation, he didn't even know that I had children.

## Planet Starbuckia:
## Wild Hair Artist Admittedly, I've met
some people at the Starbucks watering hole who have become cherished characters in my life.

My wild hair artist Kristi is one of them. I heard Kristi before I saw her. Engrossed in my book, I heard life and glorious rebellion amongst the *Starbuckians*. A woman's voice—bountiful cursing, shrewd humor and vulnerable honesty—all from one pow-er-packed little person with wild hair and tattoos galore.

Kristi became a regular for awhile. I lis-tened intently whenever she spoke because, well, she was hilarious and fascinating. She acted out her encounters with people, imitated her dog Sam, and was very, very smart, but had no idea just how brilliant she was.

After several sessions of eavesdropping, I asked her if she were a writer. She was shocked. She told me no, and that she had read only one short book in her entire life. I told her that she thought like a writer, was brilliant, observant and interesting, and that I hoped she would start writing because she had a lot to say. She was flummoxed.

**Big Hair** **Several months after moving to**
the sticks, I was depressed about the lack
of amenities that one finds in the city. I
couldn't find a genuine *hair artist* anywhere
up in the boonies. Wings from the 1970s—
à la Farrah Fawcett—and big hair, shags,
frizz-perms and bad color jobs were still en
vogue in the foothills. I needed someone
with San Francisco sensibilities.

Then I bumped into zesty Kristi from
'Bucks. She told me she was a stylist and
had just opened her own salon. I was over-
joyed. I made an appointment and discovered a fabulously avant-garde, entertaining
and giant-hearted artist. At my first appointment I told Kristi that she was the artist and
my head was her blank canvas . . . to do
whatever she wanted. She did, and I loved
it! I left her salon that day with very short
platinum hair with a swatch of black in the
front, replete with subtle touches of purple,

midnight blue and magenta that glistened like an abalone shell in the sunlight.

Almost daily, men and women stop me on the street to compliment my hair. Women say I'm brave and tell me they wish they had the courage to wear their hair the way I wear mine.

**Brave Hair** It boggles me that so many women consider it being very brave when deciding to wear certain hairstyles. Actually, it makes me sad. When just being yourself becomes an act of bravery, something is off.

The beauty of hair is that it grows back, so changing hair is a temporary and risk-free micro-adventure, a good place to begin to take chances.

When trying new things becomes un-natural, I know that my free, spontaneous nature is eroding. When fitting into the norm starts to dictate personal choices, then my heart numbs and life consists of go-ing through the motions.

For me, this usually happens when I for-get who I am and doubt my intuition, when I think others are smarter, more successful, more *fillintheblankhere*. It happens when a spirally peg tries to fit into a square hole.

**Flame**  **Every home needs flame. A fire.** Even if it's a little one, like the flame of a candle. Flame is vital. Flame is heat, radiance, movement, passion, romance, enlightenment, color and quiet.

I try to incorporate flame in my every day. A bath by candlelight. A fire in the fireplace. The inimitably warm and soothing light that can only come from fire.

Sunrise always feels like a sacred ritual to me, one in which a giant candle is lit as a benediction of light and hope for the day. Ah, *oui. Le soleil.* The ultimate flame on my life's candle.

**Fire for Sooty** I do not recall ever being called "Jennifer" by my dad. How he came up with "Sooty," I will never know.

My dad celebrated winter by building roaring fires in the fireplace. In fact, he made his fires so hot that the fireplace bricks began to crumble.

When it rained on the tin roof over the patio, I loved to read in the living room and listen to the drumming.

On occasion my dad emerged from his darkroom in the garage and said, "Sooty, you need a fire!" And then he'd build me a fire. I'd lie on the floor in front of the flames with the *rainbeat* and read to my heart's content.

**Bonfires** Bonfires are fun. Bonfires are hard to resist. They invite even extreme *perpetualmotionmachinebrains* to sit and rest. Bonfires are the perfect excuse to do nothing. Around a bonfire, people can talk . . . or not. Around a bonfire, silence is comfortable. People are often content just to stare at the flames.

I want to live a bonfire life. To be so lit up that I am a warm, comfortable place for people. Welcoming. A reason to slow down and relax. A do-nothing portal of warmth and simplicity. And I want to be hot enough to be dangerous!

Bonfires beckon. A crackling bonfire is an irresistible beacon. Ah, a beckoning beacon bonfire. Lovely alliteration.

## My Crowning Achievement I was

backpacking in torrential rain at Point Reyes National Seashore in Northern California. A few other backpackers dotted the beach. Several of these dots tried, unsuccessfully, to start a fire.

Several years prior, a friend had described to me how he had made a fire in a downpour while camping in Canada. On the beach in the rain was a good opportunity to try to do this myself, I thought.

I hunted for driftwood. I organized the pieces of wood into piles . . . tiny, slightly bigger than tiny, and on up to *prettydarnbig*.

The key is to build a Barbie-doll-sized fire first. Take the tiny, teeny pieces and arrange them in a little campfire shape. Then shield it from the wind and rain while you light it and it takes. Once you have this miniature fire going well, carefully add the next size wood pieces one at a time until that slightly larger fire is ablaze, and so forth.

It worked! In the pouring rain, my driftwood bonfire was unquenchable. Soon, the scattered dots on the beach formed a circle around my fire. My fellow travelers asked me, "*Howonearth* did you do this? We tried, but couldn't get it to light." I just smiled. I did not mention that this was my first fire in the rain.

The key to good fire building is to refuse to be in a hurry. It takes patience to build a fire, just as it does to build anything else warm and wonderful.

**Jnfr-Time** Impatience has been the bane of my existence for too long. Finally, I've learned to recognize the first signs that I am feeling impatient and refuse to go *there.* I'm rarely impatient with people. And never on the road. The type of impatience in which I specialize is impatience with the gestation time after the conception of an idea, that very important period of development and refinement before the idea is born and bears fruit.

I believe that my impatience is due, in part, to my skewed sense of time. I'm a lot like a dog where one human year equals seven dog years. From my perspective, the ratio is about the same for "*jnfr-time*," except one human month equals seven Jennifer-months.

I usually feel that things do not happen fast enough or that *nothing* is happening because I don't see immediate results. Many times, clients have thanked me for my

quick results. I stare at them blankly because it feels to me like the work has taken
an eternity to complete.

*Jnfr-time* has also led to a few glitches
in my time management regarding setting
impossible expectations for myself and my
clients regarding delivery. To help with this, I
have a little formula I use: y=2.5x, where "x"
is the amount of time I estimate the project
will require and "y" is the time it will really
take for things to wrap.

**Iris** **I had never gardened before. Twenty-**
one-years-old and newly married, I lived in a
condominium with a tiny backyard.

A friend gave me some iris bulbs from
her flower beds to plant. Very carefully, I
planted each bulb, just the way she had
instructed. The leaves appeared. They were
so strong and beautiful. But nothing else
happened. I waited. And waited.

And then I saw irises in full bloom at
the florist. As I didn't know anything about
hothouses, I immediately assumed that my
irises were defective because they hadn't
yet bloomed. I pulled all the bulbs up. There
they lay on the patio, some with their leaves
ripped off.

The friend who had given me the bulbs
stopped by. When she saw the destruction,
she exclaimed, "What the hell have you
done?" I told her why I had pulled them
up, that they were defective because they
hadn't bloomed yet. "Jennifer," she said,

"They are not supposed to bloom for another two months!"

Then I had an epiphany. (My friend Rose jokingly tells me that I have way too many epiphanies and that I'm allowed only one per day.) Patience increases our velocity. Impatience slows everything way down. I reason that if I want things—relationships, projects, learning—to flow smoothly and move full steam ahead, then I must be patient. When I am feeling anxious, impatient or pushy, I delay or obstruct good things from happening.

**Tragedy** There is absolutely nothing on earth so important that we need to honk, push, hurry, pressure, swerve, force and possibly kill to get there.

The tragedy of impatience was illustrated in the *Oakland Tribune*'s lead story one day. A car had its right-turn indicator on at an intersection. Even though the traffic light had turned green, the car was not moving. The impatient driver in the car directly behind this car—who also wanted to turn right—honked at the stationary car then swerved around it and made his right turn.

The stopped car had not proceeded because a child was crossing the street. The child was not visible to anyone but the stopped driver. The impatient driver who raced around the stopped car and made his right-hand turn hit and killed the child.

I carry this example of the fatal nature of impatience with me every single time I get in my car.

**Cake** **I like cake. Cakes are celebratory.** And pretty. Cakes are romantic. Can you imagine being sent an exquisite, elegant cake by your lover? Or fed cake by candlelight on a summer evening? Evening miniature cakes—*petits fours*—are delightful. What about a picnic with *petits fours*? What about sitting alone with a slice of cake and an espresso, overlooking the ocean? Cake holds infinite possibilities for elegance, romance and celebration.

The owner of a local bakery-café heard that I was an artist and asked to see my work. While I had several paintings ready to show, her inquiry inspired me to paint a giant cake. In fact, it's over one square meter of cake heaven.

Spreading the pink paint-frosting on the three-tiered cake, I began to feel celebratory. I decided to add some grapes that became lilac blossoms, and then some leaves. The leaves weren't quite right, though.

Someone asked if they were jalapeño pep-
pers. I didn't care. I decided not to mess
with them.

The background evolved, along with the
tablecloth. I decided to paint the tablecloth
gold to signify a rich life, and to fill the background with the colors of joy, swirls of yellow and white and blue, of music and laughter and anticipation. I decided to amuse
myself by adding one more thing: I wrote
the word *gâteau* (*cake* in French) on top of
the cake. This pleased me. A sort of private
joke. Obviously, this was a cake. To state the
obvious completely cracked me up. *Gâteau.*

The owner of the bakery came over to
choose some paintings. Interestingly, she
didn't choose the cake (probably because
of the jalapeños). So the enormous pink
gâteau now hangs in my dining room, an
everyday-reminder to celebrate life.

## My Jazz-Concert Husband  Louis

Armstrong liquefies me. Brings me to my knees. Melts me into *Jnfr-butter*. When I hear Louie, I want to make love, to dance slowly, to paint.

My son Justin is a jazz trumpeter. He loves Louie, too. When Justin solos, I can't move. Every cell in my body listens. I drink in every note. And this is not just because Justin is my son. Honest! His playing affects people. He has *it*—the ability to converse, to transport people to his colorful universe through music.

Justin has two mouthpieces for his trumpet. One I call "Dark Chocolate." The tone is rich, conversational, a bit grittier. The other I deem "Milk Chocolate" for its brighter, more *sparkly* tone.

Justin's musical expression is so full of feeling. I like to watch him play almost as much as I like to hear him play. When he is soloing, he is at the height of receptivity, intuition and beauty, at the epicenter of the pulsing heart of creation. He's one hundred percent Justin.

I was helping with Justin's high school music program's spring concert. I forewarned my fellow parent-workers that when Justin solos, I quit working and listen and that this was non-negotiable. Parents themselves, they understood completely.

I stood motionless and listened to Justin's second solo. The beauty of it was so intense that it was almost painful. A man whom I always had considered strange and obnoxious walked up, stood by my side and, without a word, put his arm around me. I lay my head on his shoulder. We listened like that for minutes. Perfection. I sent my *jazz-concert husband* an e-mail to thank him for paying attention, for being there.

And I was humbled. Before the concert, I had judged this man, put him in a nutshell and even joked about him with my son.

But he was the one who paid attention responded to the moment. Whereas before I avoided him at all costs, since that concert we have become friends in a howdy-do sort of way.

## Loneliness My jazz-concert husband

experience leads me to write about a different kind of loneliness. In my experience there is overwhelming loneliness born of fear, self-doubt and society-induced expectations. But then there is a different kind of loneliness that aches and echoes from great beauty and joy, that natural inclination to share the beauty, make love about it, celebrate it. This is a loneliness that derives from the passionate desire to share laughter and life most precious.

Sometimes I feel so happy that I start to be this kind of lonely. I feel so rich that I don't know what to do with myself. I've

learned the hard way that I mustn't seek another during these times or assume a man
is perceptive enough or willing to see and
celebrate with me. Assuming is a great way
to get into trouble. Rather, I've learned that
I must create when I'm in agony from being
so full of bliss. A poem. A painting. A cake.
Something. Anything.

**Happy Wheels** **When my children**
were quite young, each one of us had a
scooter. These scooters were the kind you
pushed with a foot like a skateboard and
steered with a handlebar. They had a little
brake on the back wheel to step on when
you got going too fast. And they folded up,
so they were easy to carry.

We lived near San Francisco Bay and
scooted everywhere. To the grocery store—
my children draped their bags over their

handlebars en route home. To the beach. To karate lessons. To school. We rarely drove. I loved it!

My best scoot ever was coming home from the grocery store on a brilliant summer day. The luscious salty sea fragrance filled the air. I was wearing a miniskirt, T-shirt and sneakers. My bag of groceries was on my handlebars and I held a magnificent bouquet of flowers across my handlebars with both hands as I steered. I sang. I whispered to myself: "I feel like a bride."

When we moved to the countryside, the distances between everything were so great and there were no sidewalks, so scooting did not work anymore. I really miss scootin'! The first thing I'll do when we move to a metro area again is to buy new scooters.

**Woohoo** Sometimes, a girl just has to let loose. I usually shop for groceries at a giant wholesale warehouse filled with huge packages of everything. One of the side benefits to shopping at this type of store is that they usually have the best-designed carts. The wheel base is wide, so they don't tip over. The handle is thick enough to get a good grip. The lower rack is a solid platform upon which to stand. Trust me—I've tested myriad stores' carts and most are not safe at high speeds.

After paying for my groceries, I wait in line for the doorman to check the receipt against the contents of the cart. Once through the door—and my children expect this now—I put my purse into the cart, check for traffic, put my right foot on the bottom rack of the cart and I'm off!

I scoot the cart as fast as I can to the car. A few yards before I reach the car, I jump off and slow to a walk. Then I look back to where my children are ambling along, pretending they are absolutely no relation to that woman riding the cart.

**Tall Ship** **I want my life to be a tall ship.**
To smell of ocean, canvas, oil and wood.
Beauty, elegance and function, with
no excess. A place for everything and
everything in its place. To sound of
adventure, water, life, craftsmanship,
creaking wood.

The Californian was making a guest
appearance in Sacramento. It was docked
on the Sacramento River. Its tall mast was
sectional. To clear the bridge over the river,
the top part of the mast disjoins then slides
down the lower half.

My friend Darci and I played hooky

from work to take a tour of *The Californian*. We walked up the ramp to the ship. Once aboard, my natural response was to close my eyes and smell the wide ocean. With my eyes still closed, I touched the canvas. The smooth wood expertly crafted. The ropes perfectly coiled. I loved the order on this ship. One of the crew told me that order was safety, that one thing out of place could kill a sailor.

*The Californian* was built for speed, to run down smugglers off the Pacific coastline. I like the idea of a life being built for speed . . . sleek, efficient and beautifully crafted.

**Africa**  **Whenever I'm in the midst of a** monumental challenge, on the verge of a soul-moving discovery, whenever I am deeply sorrowful, I long to go to Africa.

Not to the jungles, but to the desert. I long for big sky and uncomplicated living. I long to focus on survival, for everything extraneous to disappear. To be free of accumulation and complication. For the drumbeat. The voices. The color. The style. *Ubuntu* . . . that African philosophy which, as Archbishop Desmond Tutu explains, "focuses on people's relations and allegiances with each other. A person with *ubuntu* is open and available to others, affirming of others and doesn't feel threatened that others are able and good, for she has the proper self-assurance that comes from knowing that she belongs in a greater whole."

Yes, when things are tough I long for my village . . . the vast and harsh beauty of Africa in all its glorious wildness.

**Comforting Mother** I began to turn to Africa as a "Comforting Mother" when I first read *Cry of the Kalahari* by Mark and Delia Owens. The Owens lived in the heart of the Kalahari Desert for seven years. *Cry of the Kalahari* tells the story of this sojourn.

The first time I read it, I hung on every word. The second time I read it, I guzzled every word. The third time I read it, I inhaled every word. The fourth time . . . well, you get the picture.

Then I met 15-year-old Peter. He had stolen his dad's car. Had built a fire in his room. Had been taking drugs. And he had not read a book since he was eight years old.

One day, Peter's mom telephoned me. She relayed her struggles with Peter. I had just finished reading *Cry of the Kalahari* again. The Owens' story had so inspired me to think in new ways, to venture forth bravely in life, that I felt it might speak to

Peter in a similar way.

Immediately after this conversation, I drove to the bookstore, bought a copy of *Cry of the Kalahari* and headed for Peter's house.

Peter was not home. I wrote a message on the inside flap of the book, "Peter—This is a grand adventure. I thought you might enjoy it, too. Love, Jennifer." Then I left the book on his bed.

A few days later, Peter's mom called me. "Peter has not put that book down! He reads all the time. He even reads in between classes at school. And, he's going to class, which he hadn't been doing before! At dinner last night, Peter pulled out a play by Shakespeare and read it aloud to us."

No more fires in his room. No more stealing. No more drugs. No more skipping school. Rather, books. Hope. Purpose. Peace. Africa is a Comforting Mother.

**Envelope** Once upon a time, long, long ago, I had no confidence. I felt only shame and failure. I struggled to breathe my life. I was convinced that I was unlovable. And, I loved much. I fought despair. I sought every opportunity to help others, but I did not know how to help myself.

I believed the injurious brutal people who, when I was a child, treated me with disdain and disapproval. Those who sought to destroy my joy whenever I experienced success, who jeered at me, who told me how much smarter they were than I was. I listened to and sought approval from those people who never even saw or listened to me, and who continually told me I was *toowhatever* or *notenough*.

From an early age, I began my quest for a *safeplace.* I began to build a beautiful family of friends. If it weren't for this family, I would not have survived. One such friend is Beautiful Betty, a.k.a. BB.

I met Beautiful Betty when I was fifteen.

Since then, BB has been a constant lifeline of love, support and honesty. BB checked in regularly to see how I was doing, and at the time I wasn't doing well. I was out of money with no job prospects.

Soon thereafter, BB told me she had left an envelope for me that I could come pick up. When I opened her door, I saw it resting on the little table in the foyer. It was lumpy. I opened the envelope. There was a card with an angel pin on it. Inside the card was a fat check with a handwritten note from BB: "Dearest Jennifer, I am so proud of you."

I stood very still for a long time, wrapping my heart around the fact that someone was proud of me. The seed was planted and has since grown into a magnificent tree. Over the years, BB has freely poured her affection, admiration, wisdom and support into my and my children's lives. I still have that angel pin. And I don't waste any opportunity to tell my children and my friends that I am proud of them.

**Table** I have a nine-foot-long and extremely heavy mahogany refectory table. My children and I have lifted, dropped and hauled it through many moves. One leg is loose. The top is scratched and gouged. It is in desperate need of repair and refinishing. When we lived in a 600-square-foot apartment that we now refer to as "The PooPoo Palace," or alternately, "The Hovel," this table filled the entire kitchen.

But I refuse to give it up. This table is perfect for gatherings. *Everybody*—if we all squeeze a little—can fit around the table for a feast of conversation. Before a party, I just make sure that the loose leg is pushed back in where it belongs and cover it with a pink table cloth for happiness or a gold table cloth for elegance and rich friendships.

# The Best Party Ever My home smiles

when it is filled with the people I love,
when there are heaping dishes from many
countries on the table, when wine pours
and espresso is made and candles are lit.
Music and storytelling and diversity and
dancing. Heavenly!

The best party I've had to date was
an impromptu winter party. Sierra Leone,
France, India and the United States were all
amply represented.

There is nothing like a leisurely repast
with laughter and conversation. After a
fabulously drawn-out dinner (France had
brought the dessert), we migrated three
feet to the living room. We sat in a circle,
and India suggested we each tell a story
about our lives, recite a poem or sing a
song. Everyone in the circle came up with
something wonderful to share. Fabulous!

Then Sierra Leone picked up the guitar
and started to sing Bob Marley songs. We

all joined in. Sierra Leone began to make up songs. It was hilarious. Children swam in little schools throughout the house, occasionally stopping to touch base, grab a cookie or to see if we were doing anything *interesting*. India began to drum. Sierra Leone asked me to dance while the U.S. played the guitar. We waltzed, hamming it up.

The evening went on like this for a long time. Babies got sleepy. They snuggled on laps. Fussed. Fell asleep. The guests packed up their serving dishes, coats and children, said their goodbyes and left. While I have not yet traveled the world as I long to do, the world has come to me in surprising ways. And I relish every moment!

**Leopard Sharks** I was standing on a
hill looking down the slope to a vibrant
emerald green cove. The water was crystal
clear. I could see the bottom. The cove
teemed with beautiful life. I saw leopard
sharks, sea anemones, brightly colored
fish, starfish, horseshoe crabs and more. So
many fascinating and delightful creatures.
And I could sense the warmth of the water
rising to meet the air. I felt such joy!

So I ran down the hill to the cove. When
I reached the edge, I hurried to strip so that
I could dive in. Just as I was pulling my top
off, I hesitated. I had nagging thoughts that
fought the strong current of my joy. I better be careful. I seem to recall that leopard
sharks are harmless, but what if I'm mistak-
en? What if leopard sharks are predators?

These thoughts caused unbelievable
agony. Everything in me wanted to take the
plunge. But my initial slight doubt rapidly
was morphing into full fear. Soul-suffoca-
tion. A straightjacket on my wild and pure
inclinations.

I just stood there at the edge of that magnificent cove, that sea city of bountiful, fascinating life, with my shirt half off, watching everything going on in the water. Longing for it but confused and too afraid to get in.

Two days later, I Googled "leopard sharks." They eat worms and small fish buried in the sand, among other things. Harmless to humans.

Then I knew. It's too easy for me to get stuck in my own head. To think too much until my instinctual self feels foreign or untrustworthy. I feel the way I felt at the edge of that cove far too often yet, my clothes half off, ready to embrace adventure when waves of serious self-doubt begin to crash over me.

And I learn over and over again that I can trust my instincts. That when I trust them, I have wonderful adventures. Likewise, as I look back on every painful experience I've had as an adult, I recognize that there were bright red flags everywhere . . . of which I was conscious, but that I chose to ignore. My instincts were on high-alert and in full gear all along! Now that I've learned to heed them, I have nothing to fear. Next time my instincts lead me to strip and plunge in, I will. Without a second thought!

## Unloving Somebody  **Have you ever**

tried to *unlove* somebody? It's exhausting. I've reached the conclusion that once you love someone, you can never unlove him or her. The form might change, but the love remains.

Being jaded is like sandpaper to my heart. "To unlove" is deficiency language. An absence of love. An un-action. It truly isn't in me to unlove anyone who has been a teacher, either through positive means or by inverse. I know because I've tried hard to unlove a few others as a means of self-preservation. It only jumbles me up more.

While unloving doesn't work, what does work is *complete acceptance that things are the way they are.* I've caused myself a lot of anguish by determinedly clinging to *what should be but is not.*

Acceptance is the opposite of *unlove*. Acceptance gives closure without bitterness. Acceptance is love, a healthy love for oneself and a type of letting-go love for the person who has broken my heart, hurt my feelings, disappointed me or made life difficult in some other way. Acceptance is release. Acceptance is turning to the other and shouting with a smile, "Bon voyage!"

**Bon Voyage** *BonVoyage* **is a fantastic**
concept. I picture an old, jerky black-and-
white film in which I am standing on the
dock, about to christen an ocean liner by
breaking a bottle of champagne across her
bow. The offending person(s) is on the ship
waving goodbye. I smash the bottle, the
ship's horn signals and the tugboats pull the
ship away from dock and out to open sea.

I call this my *BonVoyage Methodology*.
For example, when I slip into recalling hurt-
ful comments made by a former spousal
unit, I put him on the deck of the ship about
to leave my harbor. Then I definitely crack
the bottle of champagne across the bow of
his ship—no, wait! I decide not to waste a
perfectly good bottle of champagne. I put it
in my purse for later, so that I can toast my
emancipation. But I still wave goodbye and
wish him a great trip.

Or once, when I found myself the topic
of cruel gossip amongst a group of women, I

broke a bottle of champagne across the bow of their ship to celebrate their journey apart from mine and waved as they left port.

My *BonVoyage* approach is to say, "Our journeys are separate, and we aren't going to the same destination, but I want you to have a good trip." It's very cathartic to be able to break something, too!

*BonVoyage* is my way of showing myself that I am not at the mercy of others, that I can choose different traveling companions or destinations. It helps me accept the situation, make a choice and feel kind in the process.

**Wordplay** I like to play with my words. I really like French. And I especially like to inject French phrases and words into English. One of my favorites is to write *merci* (pronounced "mair-see"), the French word for *thank you*, like this: *mer-sea*. This pleases me. *Mer* is *Sea* in French. So *mer-sea* is *sea-sea*.

Another bit of wordplay I enjoy? *Make the most out of your mots* (pronounced "mow"). In other words, "Make the most of your *words*." *Most* and *Mots* . . . so similar. Fun, don't you think?

## **Better than Fabergé** Life was

*topsyturvy*. As is often the case, when things go sideways, I turn to Rx: ART. So there I was . . . imbibing the art at the Crocker Art Museum in Sacramento when I bumped into Taylor. Taylor, a good friend, is beautiful inside and out. I refer to him as my "27-year-old hottie."

He gave me a big hug. Then he zipped out, en route to *somewhereelse*. A few minutes later, Taylor came running back into the room, handed me a smallish heavy object and said, "I want you to have this," and ran out of the room. I looked down. In my hand was a perfect marble egg, smooth and heavy. I held that egg throughout the gallery as if it held the answers to all my big questions, as the cure for my loneliness. I designated a special inside pocket of my purse my *Taylor Eichelberger Egg (T.E.E.) Pocket.*

When I arrived home that evening, I held the egg in my hand for hours as I read.

The marble warmed. That night, I fell asleep holding my egg. When I awoke, the egg lay on my pillow. I smiled. It looked as if a mysterious hen had roosted on my pillow and laid an egg during the night. Or perhaps that I had dreamt eggy dreams, symbolic of *something*, and one of them had rolled out, from wherever dreams come from, onto my pillow.

Taylor had no idea that I was having an impossibly rough time of it when he gave me the egg. Later on, I asked him what had impelled him to put that comforting piece of marble into my hand. He told me that he collects rocks and that he often likes to hold something weighty in his hand. He bought the egg for $2.70 at a rock shop. When he saw me, he just felt I needed it. He was right.

I keep my T.E.E. with me. When I start to get stressed out or feel distant from myself, I pull it from its pocket in my purse and roll it around in my hands and focus on its pleasing coolness, smoothness and weight. I feel it warming as I hold it. It is true. There are beautiful husbands and angel-friends everywhere.

**Grandma** Grandma, the only relative of mine with whom I was close, was feisty. She was an itty-bitty li'l thing with fire in her brown eyes.

When Grandma was in her early nineties, she fell and broke a hip. She needed to be in a convalescent hospital for three months while she had physical therapy. Grandma was in heaven. So many people to criticize, so little time! For example, she once gleefully exclaimed, "Look at that ol' babe in hot pants. That should be illegal. Her butt cheeks are hanging below her shorts." And, her physical therapist was a strapping young man with whom she flirted shamelessly.

I visited Grandma every weekend. And I always brought her a large chocolate milkshake from Dairy Queen. Our routine rarely varied. I walked into her room with the milkshake. She'd say, "Oh, Jennifer. I couldn't possibly drink that big thing." I'd hand it to her. And she'd suck it down *everylastdrop*.

I often jokingly referred to her as the "Philip Morris Poster Child." She smoked most of every day for eighty-four years (from age 15 to 99). The convalescent hospital didn't allow smoking. One day I asked Grandma if it was difficult not to smoke for such an extended period of time. She looked surprised. "Not at all, Jennifer. I am not addicted." I asked her *whyonearth* she smoked then. She replied, "I smoke when I am bored."

Evidently, she was not bored at the convalescent facility. In fact, I suspected she was having the time of her life. People everywhere—much more interaction than she had seen in decades—and the human touch she craved but was too proud to ask for.

When she returned home, she resumed her ritual of smoking.

**A Few Months Short** By the time she turned 95, Grandma had shrunken so much that when I hugged her, she only came up to my rib cage. She lived on her own until one week before she died—in Arizona—in the most boring retirement development in the world. Decorative rock and racially-insulting statues of sombrero-wearing Mexicans taking siestas with their donkeys. No children. No signs of life. The entire neighborhood always seemed deserted, with the exception of momentary rustles of activity when someone pulled his Buick out of the garage or ventured out on the front porch to water a plant.

Grandma had fallen and lay on the floor in her utility room for 36 hours. A neighbor called 911 when she noticed that Grandma hadn't been retrieving her newspaper from the driveway. During the ambulance ride to the hospital, Grandma said, "Damn, I wanted to make it to 100." She was 99 years old.

Grandma spent her last week in a hospice in Arizona, in and out of consciousness. By this time, I had moved back to California. And I was in anguish because I could not be there with her. I didn't have the money for the airfare. I had a new job. No childcare. So instead, I talked with her many times each day via telephone.

The hospice worker held the phone to Grandma's ear, even when she was unconscious. Whenever Grandma heard my voice, she immediately regained consciousness and responded to me. She and the children had several short conversations. They were able to say their goodbyes.

I am immensely grateful for the hospice care Grandma received. It is still difficult for me that I wasn't there to stroke her hair and hold her hand that last week. I miss her.

**Rent-a-Dad** Sometimes I really feel my singleness. Most of these times are stressful moments in parenting, those times I feel I need backup or, at least, a break. Even someone to help me see the humor in the situation.

I have three teenagers. My daughter Aimee knows how to drive. The boys do not. And, frankly, I do not feel up to the task of being a co-pilot for a baby-driver ever again. I've not recovered from Aimee yet.

I'd be a gazillionaire if I could create a rent-a-dad website. I'd rent a dad to spend six months in the car with my neophyte driver-child. To painfully go through the terrifying process with each child when he stops the car on a blind curve on the highway because he missed the off-ramp. Or when his confidence exceeds his skill and he drives too fast, and then gets angry because I told him to slow down.

I asked Aimee if I could share my experience of her first time behind the wheel. She thinks it's funny, too, now, and gave me her blessing. She had just acquired her driver's permit. She was seated behind the wheel. I asked her to drive me down our private road to the mailboxes at the bottom of the hill. She moved the car forward, no problem. But, at the first hairpin turn, she began to panic. The road turned abruptly left, but we continued to head straight. I instructed her to turn. She turned the wheel, but then straightened it out again right away, rather than completing the turn. We crept forward slowly, heading for our neighbor's field. "Get back on the road!" I yelled. She froze. I grabbed the wheel and yanked up on the emergency brake. Upset, she cursed, called our car names and told me that it was all my fault. Sigh.

We both calmed down. Then I asked her *allaboutit*. She had panicked because the Toyota emblem on the steering wheel had turned when the wheel had turned and she thought that the emblem needed to be straight up at all times. We cleared that little misunderstanding up. Aimee is a great driver now. But there is no way in hell I want to go through that again two more times. There has to be a rent-a-dad someplace!

**Trendsetter**  When Aimee was first learning to park the car, she would circle the parking lot several times. She passed up many good spots to find the one that was *straightahead* so she didn't have to turn into the spot. On her maiden voyage to a more crowded city, parking, even in a lot, was more challenging. The spaces were smaller.

The shopping plaza parking lot was fairly empty. After much deliberation, Aimee chose her space. Or I should say that she chose her "spaces." She parked the way a person with a DeLorean would park, across two parking spaces so no one hits the sides of his fancy-pantsy car. This was unintentional, however. We have an elderly Toyota Camry.

I choose my battles carefully and decided that she had made so much progress driving that morning that I would not have her park the car again. Besides, there were only a few cars in the lot.

We went grocery shopping. When we came out of the store, the parking lot was full. At least six other drivers, rather than skipping a space beside our car and parking properly, had parked parallel to our car, matching Aimee's parking *style*. My daughter the trendsetter!

## Beauteous Maximus *Gluteous*
*maximus not*. Rather, beauteous maximus!
I *graffitied* my jeans. Underneath the back
pockets, I wrote *Beauteous Maximus*. This
delights me. I like things written across the
behind. They draw attention to it.

A graffitied bottom is an animated
billboard when the wearer of such graffiti
walks. It's irreverent. It's sassy. *Beauteous
Maximus* celebrates a woman's curvy body.

You'd be amazed at how many women
perk up when they read my ass. Sometimes,
they ask me if I will graffiti their jeans, too.
They bring their jeans to me, I graffiti them
with glee, put a big bow on the package and
return them transformed.

On occasion, I catch a man trying to
read my bottom. Only he's trying to do it on
the sly. It's really funny. It's so socially incor-
rect to stare at a woman's butt, but what if
there's something there to read?

**Lullaby**  Over the years, I developed a
very destructive habit. Just before I fell
asleep each night, I'd go through my
extremely long list of everything I did not
accomplish that day.

Where did this bizarre behavior come
from? This deficiency-approach? This regret-
mania? What better way to establish the
feeling of being *neverenough*? I could practi-
cally hear the "Song of the Volga Boatmen"
playing in the background—a song written
by Mily Balakirev and sung by barge haulers
on the Volga River in Russia . . . a song used
as background music for different scenarios
with the theme of unremitting toil or devo-
tion to duty . . . a song used to escalate the
feeling of portending doom or despair—as I
took daily account of my non-success.

So I decided not to do this anymore.
Now, before I close my eyes for the night,
I think about all that I accomplished that
day and the really good things I learned and

experienced. After singing this new lullaby for just a short while, my entire being
feels lighter and more open to joy. And I am
beginning to be much more realistic about
how successful I really am each day. Very
*merci beaucoup*. *Mer-sea*.

**Pulpit** **A friend and I were invited to sail**
in San Francisco Bay in a beautifully crafted
wooden sailboat. The gentleman had made
the entire boat himself. In his backyard, no
less.

When the boat was finished, he realized
that it wouldn't fit through either opening
between his and his neighbors' houses. So
he had to rent a crane to lift the boat up out
of his backyard, over his house and onto the
trailer on the street.

At the bow, which is the front of this
boat, he had constructed a kind of pulpit

out of stainless steel piping. The pulpit extended over the water. When he was giving us a tour of his boat, he explained that he harnessed in to ride the pulpit. I asked him if I could ride in the pulpit. He strapped me in.

I stayed there for the entire excursion! Bliss! Freedom! I felt like the figurehead of an ancient ship. A bird soaring on life. On my stomach over the water flying along the San Francisco coastline, I felt *purejoy*.

I knew why it's called the pulpit. From it comes the very best kind of sermon.

**Yalla, Baby!**  The more I write, the fuller I feel. The fuller I feel, the more I remember to write about. *A Woman's Mind Half Naked* is a mobius strip of love. I could go on forever. But if I did that, I'd never get to *A Woman's Mind Full Monty* or *A Woman's Mind in Business Casual* or whatever my next book will be titled. And this book would be so heavy it wouldn't be light anymore—shedding light, delightful, lighthearted or any other kind of "light."

Yes, it's time to stop writing this book and start a new one. You've been with me every step of the way. *Mer-sea.*

My deepest desire for *A Woman's Mind Half Naked* is that it makes you laugh. That it inspires you to look with boundless gratitude at your amazing, rich experiences and heart. And that you know we are all in this together.

*Yalla*, baby!
*("Forward march" in Arabic or "pas de stop" en français)*
Love

# **Jennifer Ann Gordon . . .**

**Whether Jennifer Ann Gordon is speaking** to groups or busy writing up a storm, she knows how to have fun and to live life deliciously.

A captivating speaker, Jennifer playfully interacts with her audience and connects with people of all ages to entertain, inspire and heal. From soirees to large events, Jennifer relishes them all and loves being on stage. Her genuine warmth, mischievousness and fresh perspective on life delights her audiences and inspires them all to *get their sassy on*.

Jennifer is passionate about entrepreneurship. She has been a guest lecturer at

California State University at Sacramento and a guest teacher for the Sacramento Entrepreneurship Academy (SEA). Jennifer has served on the board of directors of SEA from 2007 to the present, two of those years heading the marketing committee. She also oversaw SEA's annual showcase committee and co-directed and co-produced SEA's recruitment video. And in 2009, Jennifer founded "CONFIDENCE for Women Who Lead," an international women's leadership program focused on "voice, innovation and language" as the three primary colors from which all the other colors of leadership are made.

Regardless of the type of project, Jennifer takes writing seriously. Knowing well the impact that both thoughts and words have on the people in our world, she pays acute attention to the underlying thoughts, concepts and aims of a project *before* it takes form in words. She has produced a broad range of published professional work—from *Voxeo's Voice eXtensible Mark-Up Language Programmers' Guide* to her essay in *The Future of Innovation*.

Jennifer has extensive experience consulting with and writing for start-ups in the United States, Canada and Europe. She has also written for marketing, brand identity and website firms on behalf of their clients. From blogging, reader-friendly technical writing, ghostwriting and company profiles to writing website copy and banner ads, Jennifer's solid body of commercial writing runs the gamut.

Currently, Jennifer is focusing on her series of *A Woman's Mind* books, including *A Woman's Mind Full Monty* and *A Woman's Mind in Business Casual*.

**Join Jennifer!** Jennifer invites you to join her on her never-ending journey of inspiration and self-discovery! She is available for book club events (in person or by phone), women's workshops, empowerment seminars and whatever mischief you have in mind! An entertaining speaker, Jennifer can tailor her presentation to meet your organization's needs. Contact her at www.AWomansMindHalfNaked.com or through her publisher: Publishing Syndicate, 916-987-5519.